FEEDING PONIES

A group of Shetland Pony mares grazing a medium-quality paddock.

FEEDING PONIES

WILLIAM C. MILLER, F.R.C.V.S., F.R.S.E.

Till recently, Director, Equine Research Station,
Newmarket

J. A. ALLEN & CO.

LONDON

First published in 1968 by
J. A. Allen & Co. Ltd
1 Lower Grosvenor Place
London SW1W 0EL

SBN 85131 211 X

Printed in Great Britain by
Butler & Tanner Ltd
Frome and London

CONTENTS

Chapter   *page*

INTRODUCTION   1

    Freedom of movement. Water. Exercise. What is a pony?

1 ANATOMY OF DIGESTIVE SYSTEM   6

    Mouth and throat—teeth, tongue, gullet. Stomach. Small intestines. Caecum. Colon and rectum. Resting periods.

2 THE FOODSTUFFS   16

    Composition and functions. Carbohydrates. Proteins. Fats. Fibres. Minerals. Vitamins—sources and functions.

3 FEEDING OF PONIES   24

    Grass: Variations in quality. Surplus growth. Acreages per pony. 'Hay-on-the-stalk.' Varieties of grasses. Grasses of good, medium, poor and useless quality. Strains. Methods of grazing. Selective grazing. Alternation of paddocks.

    Hays: Seeds hays, meadow hays. Amounts to feed.

    Oats: To judge good oats. Weight per bushel. Whole versus crushed oats.

    Bran: Bran mashes. To make a bran mash. Other mashes.

4 DIFFERENCES IN CANADA AND
   THE U.S.A.   51

5 CUBES AND CUBE-FEEDING   54
   Different ways of feeding cubes.

6 AMOUNTS TO FEED   58
   General considerations. Daily amounts.

ILLUSTRATIONS

page

Frontispiece Shetland Pony mares grazing

Figure 1 Positions of the incisor teeth   8

       2 Median section of horse's head   9

       3 Principal parts of the alimentary canal 12

       4 Differences between rigid and soft tubes 14

       5 Differences in types of oats   36

  6–11 Samples of oats, bran, etc.   40–45

INTRODUCTION

Many young people possess ponies today who have no little book to guide them and whose parents or friends are themselves not really very sure how a pony should be fed and managed. Too often one hears: 'Oh, I can turn the pony out into an orchard, or a piece of rough grass'; or 'I can get a local farmer to let it graze along with his cows'; or something like that. So many people seem to think 'some grass' and 'some hay' are all that a pony needs.

To understand something of what is in reality a very complex physiological process—namely, the conversion of grass, hay, oats, bran and other foods into bone, muscle, blood and all the other tissues which make up the pony's body—there must be an understanding of simple anatomy and physiology of the horse, and some idea of what the food-stuffs consist and what use the horse can make of them. Then there must be an understanding of practical methods of feeding: what should be done and what should be avoided.

First, however, something must be discussed about horses generally: where they live in the wild state and how they manage to feed themselves on the prairies, the wide pampas, the savannah countries, or the dry arid stretches of almost desert-type country.

FREEDOM OF MOVEMENT

The horse is not a forest animal. It has developed throughout thousands of years as a creature which inhabits the open grass country where it can roam over wide stretches of

1

different kinds of country—the richer moist valleys, the hilly rocky slopes and the wide flat plains.

Freedom of movement of this sort is essential to the horse and its cousins, like the zebra, the kiangs of Asia and the wild asses. This freedom is needed for two reasons: (i) to enable it to see its enemies from a long way off and to be able to gallop away out of danger when pursued; and (ii) to ensure that it can eat a great variety of grasses, herbage plants and even shrubs so as to ensure an adequate intake of the many food ingredients—fibre, starches, proteins which are flesh-forming, minerals which form bone, and vitamins which are essential for life itself—all of which the horse needs.

In many places where herds of wild horses live, some parts are richer in some of these essentials and in other parts they are absent or deficient. In the upland areas minerals are in poor supply in the soil and the plants grown on them have only small amounts in consequence. In the richer valleys the mineral supply is greater, partly because the minerals from the hills become washed down by the rains into the valleys and are deposited in the soil there. Plants, grasses, etc., grow in richer profusion, and shrubs and trees grow naturally where there is moisture and shelter. Visits to the richer areas are generally of only short duration, since in them enemies may lurk, but the grass is rich and even short grazing periods supply nutritive substances lacking on the dry hills. In times of long and severe droughts the grass-lands on the hills and plains become withered and dry and of less value to the horse, but the valley areas contain water and better food.

It will be understood that the wild horse eats many different kinds of shrubs, grasses and plants growing in different kinds of soil, and consequently picks up a little of one thing in one place and a little of another elsewhere. The sum total of this type of 'extensive grazing' is that all the many nutritional requirements are fulfilled and in the wild state nearly all horses and ponies are fit and strong, neither too fat nor too poor, and can survive under conditions which may seem harsh and inadequate to us.

An awareness of these fundamentals is of help in appreciating some of the nutritive requirements of ponies kept under the very different and quite artificial conditions of modern society.

WATER

The digestive system has one absolutely essential requirement—*water*—if it is to perform its work properly. A further reason for freedom of movement is so that twice daily, usually at dawn and dusk, the herds can come down from the high lands to drink at streams, lakes, rivers or water-holes along with other 'grass-eating' wild animals. In the wild state observers have noted that horses will travel long distances trotting and walking to drink, nearly always in the morning and evening, and seldom is this regular routine upset without suffering.

EXERCISE

The next factor of very great importance is exercise. Horses of all kinds must have exercise. They are so constructed that the acts of walking, trotting or cantering perform essential parts in stimulating movements of the digestive system, and therefore in encouraging good nutrition and absorption of food principles. Every time a foot comes to the ground when a horse or pony moves, big thin-walled veins in the feet are squeezed and the blood circulation is improved. Further, movement especially at fairly fast paces increases the efficiency of the expansion and contraction of the chest and consequently of the lungs as well. More fresh air is inspired and more harmful gases are got rid of. The older (and fatter) a pony is, the more it needs exercise every day.

The wild horse takes a great deal of exercise every day of its life. The foal is up onto its feet in about 15 to 20 minutes after birth, follows its mother rather awkwardly at first, but in 3 to 4 hours can walk quite well and at 1 day old is able to trot along with the herd even if rather slowly. At $2\frac{1}{2}$ to 3 weeks old the foal can gallop and keep up quite well with the older animals for distances up to 2 or 3 miles at a time.

Various estimates have been made of the distances a herd of wild horses regularly travels each day when not disturbed. Some say 12 miles, some 20 miles and some more than this. Doubtless the distances covered will vary very much according to the region and many other circumstances.

The important thing to remember is that all horses, including childrens' ponies, must have adequate exercise daily; if not, all the latest knowledge about feeding and nutrition and physiology is doomed to be nearly useless and the pony cannot remain really healthy and fit.

WHAT IS A PONY?

To different people a pony means different things. Many would say a pony is just a small horse, but this does not mean very much. There is a sort of general understanding that a pony should not measure more than $14\frac{1}{2}$ hands high and this is perhaps as good as any other guide.

Ponies belong to many different breeds. The most important British breeds are the Shetland (the smallest), Welsh Mountain, Fells and Dales, Exmoor, Dartmoor, New Forest,

Highland Pony and the Hackney Pony. Some would also include the Connemara and the Highland Garron, but these often measure more than the above $14\frac{1}{2}$-hand limit and they are often of a heavier body type with heavier and stronger legs than would be typically expected in a pony to be used essentially as an animal to be ridden. They are more like little cart horses, and crofters often use them for draught purposes.

Many ponies today are bred by crossing a mare of one of the pedigree pony breeds with a stallion of another pony breed, or with one of the smaller Arab or Thoroughbred stallions. The small Thoroughbred sire tends to change some of the good characters of a pony breed in the following ways: the body, legs and head are usually fined down and the cross-bred is more showy; temperamentally the crosses become more excitable, firey and less docile, needing rather firmer management and better horsemanship; the typical hardiness, strength, staying power, docility and intelligence of most pony breeds are reduced or even largely lost, but capacity for speed over relatively short distances is improved. There are thus some advantages and some disadvantages in using the small Thoroughbred sire to produce a first-cross riding pony.

The use of an Arab stallion onto a pony mare does not have quite the same effects, and there are many good useful ponies produced by this crossing.

One of the cardinal principles which has to be constantly borne in mind is that the more highly bred a pony is, the better feeding it requires, while the strong, hardy smaller pony, perhaps particularly the mountain and moorland types, has a better digestive efficiency, is inherently capable of living on less food than a highly bred one, can tolerate bad weather better, and indeed is very liable to become far too fat when fed upon a ration which is satisfactory for a pedigree, more refined or highly bred pony of the same weight.

It will be appreciated that it is very difficult in consequence to write dogmatically and precisely about feeding, when there are so many different kinds of small horses included in the rather vague comprehensive word 'pony'. Indeed it would be an almost impossible task were it not that everyone who keeps a pony must use all his intelligence and common sense. It is possible to offer guidance in the principles of pony feeding; it is not possible to lay down hard-and-fast rules, schedules or precise rations to meet all conditions and to feed all ponies.

Chapter 1

ANATOMY OF
THE DIGESTIVE SYSTEM

To understand something of the complex mechanism of digestion, brief accounts of the essential parts of the digestive tract are necessary, with indications of the work they carry out, i.e. their functions.

THE MOUTH AND THROAT

The horse is herbivorous and requires strong teeth and jaws to chew the roughage in its food. Its jaws are comparatively long, to allow room for the large molar (cheek) teeth, and have powerful cheek muscles.

The *incisor teeth* within the lips are entirely used for prehension, i.e. cropping, grazing and 'prehending' the food. The incisors in the upper and lower jaw should meet each other level and precisely, when seen from the side. The upper jaw should not be 'overshot', which is commoner than many people realise; nor should it be 'undershot'. Both these faults are a handicap in grazing and should be avoided when buying a pony.

The *molar teeth* of the horse are big and strong and of much greater length than they appear to be, since about three-quarters of them are buried in the tooth sockets. Each is composed of folded enamel, which is very hard and constructed to reduce the friction of constant grinding of food. As they slowly wear, each tooth grows and is gradually

7

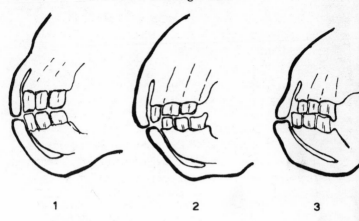

1   **2**   **3**

Fig. 1. Diagram of the position of three incisor teeth of a pony seen from the side. The most anterior one is the *central*, the next the *lateral*, and that situated posteriorly is the *corner* incisor in each diagram.

1 is the normal appearance, in which the upper and lower teeth meet each other properly. 2 shows an '*overshot*' upper jaw. The upper central incisor does not meet the corresponding lower tooth and normal wear does not occur. Similarly the lower corner incisor does not meet the opposite tooth and a sort of 'hook-like' projection of unworn tooth can be seen. In 3 there is an '*undershot*' jaw. The lower central incisor is not in wear, nor is the upper corner, which latter develops a so-called 'hook'.

Ponies with mouths as in 2 and 3 are handicapped in grazing and may lose condition unless the teeth are reduced by rasping at perhaps 12 to 15 month intervals.

protruded further from its socket enough to compensate for this natural wear.

The *tongue*, as in the human being, controls the food in the mouth during chewing and its root takes part in swallowing. It is extremely sensitive and has many taste glands which enable pleasant or unpleasant tastes to be appreciated.

The *throat* is where the air passages and the digestive

passages cross each other. The shape of the throat is rather like a funnel opening into the gullet, which is a narrow tube leading down into the stomach.

Food, after chewing and mixing with saliva in the mouth, is separated into little balls by the back of the tongue, and these are passed back into the throat and on into the gullet. The swellings made in the gullet by each little ball of food can normally be seen during feeding on the left side of the neck passing down quite rapidly to disappear at the base of the neck into the chest cavity, on their way to the stomach.

The *stomach* of a pony holds about 2 to $2\frac{1}{2}$ gallons, but its walls are very elastic and it can expand to some extent.

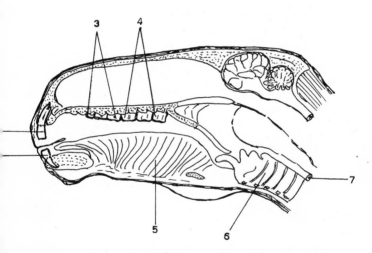

Fig. 2. Median section of horse's head. 1, upper incisor teeth; 2, lower incisor teeth; 3, first three upper right pre-molar teeth; 4, upper right molar teeth; 5, the root of the tongue; 6, larynx; 7, the gullet or oesophagus, which passes food to the stomach. Where bone is sectioned it is stippled.

Part of it is lined with digestive mucous membrane possessing digestive glands and part by a tough, almost horny membrane possessing no glands.

The food is rapidly mixed with the digestive juices secreted by the glands, and is constantly being kneaded by contractions of the muscles of the stomach wall. The fluids are pressed out of the now pulpy food, and these are rapidly passed into the *small intestine,* where they are further mixed with bile and pancreatic juices and with the juices of the small intestine itself. Much further mixing and movement occur in the 70 feet or so of the small intestine and a good deal of absorption into the lymph system takes place in this organ.

From time to time the more fibrous portions of the food are passed from the stomach into the small intestine and hurried through this tube into the *caecum* of the large intestine. This is a large, capacious, more or less triangular sac, with entrance and exit quite near each other. In a pony its capacity is about 8 to 10 gallons, but it is greatly distensible and it may hold more or less. It plays a very important part in churning and kneading the food, far more efficiently than the stomach, and holds the more fibrous portions of the food for up to 24 or even 36 hours at a time. The constant kneading and churning movements are aimed at very thorough mixing with further secretions from the caecal glands, and they control fermentation and gas formation. It is a very important organ and when something goes wrong it is subject to packing of food (impaction) and obstructive colic.

The foodstuffs, whether they are fibrous like hay and the husks of oats, or succulents like grass, apples or carrots, are now thoroughly softened and have been acted upon by the enzymes so that most of the digestible portions have been changed. They are soft and watery, and the nutritive materials, whether proteins, starches, sugars, fats, minerals or other substances, are dissolved and become fluid. These are known as the 'nutritive metabolites' and constitute the form in which all the essential food substances are extracted from the foods eaten and absorbed into the blood stream. The remainder, which is not digestible, is also present, usually as 'woody fibre'. This is passed onwards into the colon and rectum.

The *large colon*, which follows the caecum, continues and extends the process of conversion to fluid metabolites. Some of these are absorbed from the large colon, but most are passed on into the *small colon*. Here the foodstuffs are firmly squeezed and pressed upon by the powerful circular muscles, so that they are separated into (*a*) fluids containing metabolites and (*b*) an insoluble indigestible fraction (mostly 'woody fibre') which is kneaded into small roundish balls to be passed into the rectum and then evacuated as droppings or faeces to the outside (see Fig. 3).

This is a very brief and simplified account of equine digestion. It is quite different from the process in man or any other animal, and some understanding of it will greatly help in an appreciation of many of the principles which govern good feeding. It must be appreciated that the whole process of digestion is a continuous one taking place day and night. It is always subject to outside influences. When a horse is fevered, shocked, frightened, hurt, very tired, ill or has not had food or water for a long time, or when sudden changes in feeding stuffs or in the system of feeding take place, then the smooth, regular working of the digestive organs is upset. Indigestion, gas formation, impaction or other disturbance, with perhaps attacks of colic, is very liable to result. There are lessons to be learnt from a knowledge of these matters,

B

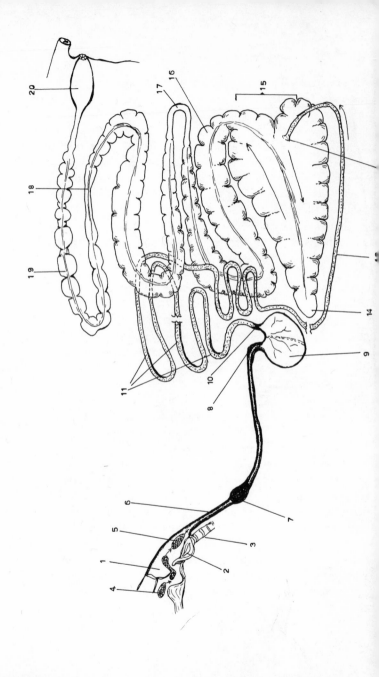

Fig. 3. Diagram to illustrate the principal parts of the alimentary canal of the horse. The intestines have been unravelled and greatly simplified to enable the progress of food during its passage from throat to rectum to be followed.

The throat region: 1, pharynx; 2, larynx; 3, beginning of windpipe (trachea); 4 and 5, ball of food in its passage from the mouth into the gullet.

The thickwalled gullet: 6, first portion in the neck; 7, a ball of food passing down onwards through the chest towards the stomach; 8, the opening into the stomach with thickened strong walls.

The stomach: 9, the main bulk of the stomach, capacity in pony 2 to $3\frac{1}{2}$ gallons; 10, the pylorus, a valve which controls the exit of food into the small intestine.

The intestines: 11, the coils of the small intestine, about 50 feet long in the pony. They lie partly among the other abdominal organs. The length has been interrupted in two places. 12, the last part of the small intestine which opens at 13 into the large caecum; 14, apex of the caecum, and 15, the base of this organ. 16 is the origin of the large colon, and 17 is the narrow pelvic flexure where stoppage or impaction may readily take place, leading to colic. 18 is where the small colon begins; 19 shows one of the saccules of the small colon which squeezes the food and forms the faeces into the characteristic little formed balls, ultimately to be accumulated in 20, the rectum, from whence they are passed to the outside.

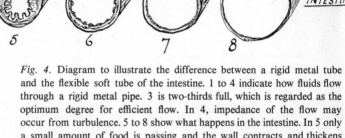

Fig. 4. Diagram to illustrate the difference between a rigid metal tube and the flexible soft tube of the intestine. 1 to 4 indicate how fluids flow through a rigid metal pipe. 3 is two-thirds full, which is regarded as the optimum degree for efficient flow. In 4, impedance of the flow may occur from turbulence. 5 to 8 show what happens in the intestine. In 5 only a small amount of food is passing and the wall contracts and thickens with the mucous membrane thrown into folds; 6 and 7 show increasing degrees of distension, the diameter of the tube is increasing and mucosal folds are obliterated. 8 shows maximum optimum distension with the walls thin, mucosal folds absent and the diameter considerably increased. If dilatation occurs beyond this, pain or discomfort is felt.

which will be referred to in later sections. The simple diagrams may help to make clear some details which are very difficult to describe in words.

It should also be appreciated that the pony's stomach is quite small and cannot hold a very large feed eaten greedily. Tests have shown that a normal pony eating its food quickly will fill up its stomach in about 20 minutes. After that the rate of feeding slows down. Some food must leave the stomach before any more can be eaten. Ponies kept indoors must be fed little and often rather than be given large amounts only once daily. When out at grass the pony will settle to graze slowly and regularly, and a balance between the amount of food coming into and leaving the stomach is quickly established.

THE IMPORTANCE OF RESTING

Rest is very important. Only when a horse or pony has been grossly starved previously will it eat or graze without stopping for long periods at a time. The normal behaviour is for a pony to graze for about 3 hours (or less) at a time. Then it will stop and may stand resting, perhaps under a tree in the shade, or may lie down and give the impression of being half-asleep. It may rest for only 20 minutes or up to 2 hours or so, but neither a horse nor a pony will stay down lying out flat on its side for much more than 20 to 30 minutes at a time. After this it will rise, stretch itself and then remain standing for a further period. If very tired it may lie down again soon after having stood up.

These resting periods, whether at grass or indoors in a loose box, are necessary for good digestion to take place. During them the final digestion of the food in the large intestine is taking place, and the residual material is being passed on into the rectum. Most ponies after a resting period will evacuate their faeces almost immediately after they have risen to their feet and finished their normal stretch.

So far as possible indoor ponies should be allowed some period of at least an hour when they can rest undisturbed during each day. This may usually be arranged most conveniently after the mid-day feed in the early afternoon. When out at grass for the day they will choose their own time to rest, and should be left alone.

Chapter 2

THE FOODSTUFFS

COMPOSITION AND FUNCTIONS

Practically all foods, and certainly all those normally used for feeding horses, consist of carbohydrates, proteins, fats, fibre, minerals, water and some vitamins. These are collectively called the 'proximate principles' of foods, but this name, though convenient, is not really of much help in understanding feeding.

Carbohydrates include the soluble sugars, the more complex sugars, the starches and fibre. They are composed of carbon, hydrogen and oxygen, combined together in many different proportions. All carbohydrates which can be digested have to be broken down by enzyme action from their complex original composition into simpler and simpler compounds until they become soluble sugars, and as such they are absorbed from the intestinal walls and enter the circulation. They are carried throughout the body to be utilised by body cells of all sorts. Most of the sugars are utilised for nourishing the cells and producing heat and energy. Any surplus to the body's requirements is converted into fat and other substances, and stored. Ponies, as distinct from bigger horses, have normally a very efficient digestive system and, often being greedy feeders, are very prone to become too fat, particularly when they are unable to expend enough energy in adequate exercise, and have a regular excess of the products of the digestion of carbohydrates, because of too much food.

16

It must be emphasised that muscles need sugars to enable them to contract and perform work, not protein-rich foodstuffs, a point which far too many people fail to understand.

The typical carbohydrate foods of the horse are, of course, oats, bran, hay and grass, particularly the coarse fibrous grass which is characteristic of autumn and winter-time grazings. This is what is often called 'hay on the stalk'.

Proteins are the so-called 'flesh-forming' substances. They have complex chemical compositions, but all contain nitrogen in addition to carbon, hydrogen, oxygen and other substances. They are sometimes referred to as the 'nitrogenous foods'. The amount of protein present in any foodstuff varies greatly. Beans and peas are the richest, and poor old hay has the lowest values. Oats contain from about 8 per cent in inferior samples up to about 10 per cent or more in best 'potato' oats, usually grown in Scotland or the north.

All proteins, and there are many hundreds, are essentially composed of amino acids. There are only some 28 of these known, but every protein is made up of them combined in different proportions. The amino acids can be compared to bricks and building stones of different kinds and sizes. There are all sorts of ways of combining bricks and stones to build all kinds of houses, sheds, walls and so on. Similarly with amino acids: an enormous number of different kinds of proteins can be built up by different combinations of amino acids of different sizes and shapes combined in different proportions.

During the digestion of proteins, the complex substances are broken down progressively to simpler and simpler compounds, until finally absorption occurs, principally in the form of amino acids. (As during demolitions, the houses are broken down into big blocks, and then finally into bricks and stones.)

In the horse's intestinal system this protein breakdown is brought about by the enzyme action of the digestive juices, aided by certain useful bacteria which are present in the alimentary canal and called proteolytic.

Proteins have a very important part to play in the body. The amino acids after absorption are recombined with each other and are used in growth and repair of the wear and tear which all body cells suffer. They are not used up in muscular exercise, and a horse fed too much protein does not become stronger or faster in consequence. On the other hand a growing foal or yearling must have an adequate amount of protein if it is to grow properly, building up its muscles normally to their full size, and not be small or stunted when it is adult.

Some of the protein intake is unable to be used by the horse's tissues and, after undergoing a change, is filtered out of the blood stream by the kidneys and passed out in the form of nitrogen compounds in the urine. Useful protein fed in excess of requirements is altered in character, loses its nitrogen and then is stored as a fat reserve, perhaps to be called upon again during a period of food shortage or extreme cold, to provide energy and heat.

Fats are not utilised by horses to anything like the extent that carbohydrates and proteins are used. The horse, in comparison with the pig or the whale, is a very poor digester of fats. This is reflected in the traditional foods used for horses: oats only contain about 4 per cent of fat; hay contains very little indeed but some is present in ripe hay seeds. Green fresh grass contains hardly any fat and only about 4 per cent is present even in bran. On the other hand, some artificial horse or pony cubes tend to contain too much fat and because of this are not always digested as well as they should be.

The horse has a peculiarity in comparison with other animals in so far as its fat depôts are concerned. These fat depôts are laid down mainly around the kidneys and in the abdominal cavity, and act as reservoirs of energy and heat for use in times of scarcity. In the horse, the type of fat is based on linoleic acid, and this is the type present in linseeds; to some extent this indicates one reason why linseed mashes, linseed drinks, linseed tea, and so on are so suitable for horses.

Fibre is the hard tough material in hay, straws, the outer husk of oats, etc. It is of two kinds: one which is digested and one which is not. The former is known as *cellulose* and its derivatives; and the latter is *lignin*. The most typical lignin is wood, and lignin is often referred to as 'woody fibre'.

Both digestible fibre and woody fibre are needed by the horse for efficient digestion, and are most important. If concentrated foods only are fed to a horse without any fibre, the material becomes packed into a porridge-like mass first, and then as the more fluid parts are removed by the squeezing and kneading movements of the stomach and intestines the porridge becomes doughy and then like putty. The digestive juices cannot penetrate, digestion becomes indigestion; fermentation begins, which is practically speaking the same as decomposition and rotting or decay. This leads to complicated toxin production, gas formation with dilatation of the bowel, pain and illness.

If this same concentrated food, perhaps cubes, is well mixed with the fibre in hay, the woody particles break up the pasty mass in the stomach and intestines, and normal digestion takes place.

There is a further reason. Fibre maintains a certain

amount of space distension inside the bowel and stimulates the normal movements which are essential to digestion. These movements are called *peristalsis*—a word which implies constant contraction and expansion of the gut wall, to move the foodstuffs backwards and forwards, churning and mixing the food very thoroughly, squeezing out the fluids and absorbing them, and passing the indigestible residues gradually onwards to be evacuated from the rectum as droppings, dung or faeces eventually (see Fig. 3).

The great importance of an adequate amount of fibre in a pony's rations must never be forgotten.

Minerals are needed by the horse for two principal reasons: to build up and maintain the bony skeleton, and to provide a proper mineral balance in the blood stream. Since the blood is distributed to every cell in the body (except teeth, horn, hair and the cornea of the eye), it carries to them the minerals they need for life and activity.

The bone-forming minerals are principally calcium (Ca), phosphorus (P) and magnesium (Mg), but small amounts (traces) of others such as iron, iodine, manganese, copper, cobalt, etc., are required by the body and are present in the bone marrow, chiefly in association with the blood.

The bones are formed first from a framework of soft fibrous tissue and cartilage, in the spaces of which the minerals are gradually deposited until a solid hard mass is built up by a very complicated physiological process. All the minerals in the skeleton must come from the horse's food. The mare provides the young embryo with what it needs from her own food or her own bone reserves, and after birth the foal has to obtain the minerals it needs from the mare's milk first and then from the various foods, grass plants, manger foods, etc., which it eats.

Roughly speaking, most of the calcium comes from the

blades and stems of hay, and the phosphorus comes from seeds and grains. Some magnesium comes from each of these. Best-quality hay containing about one-third clover or other legumes is the richest source of calcium, especially when grown on good soil containing plenty of lime, while oats, bran, peas and beans are good sources of phosphorus and magnesium.

However, there are many areas of the country, where ponies are grazed, where the mineral contents in the soil are low or poor, and in these it is often necessary (or very advisable) to supply a balanced mineral mixture, particularly for foals, yearlings, brood mares both while pregnant and while suckling their foals, and for all young ponies which are still growing, but the adult mature pony in such areas also requires some minerals daily (see p. 20).

The horse also requires a supply of other chemicals, such as sodium, chlorine, potassium and sulphur, but except for sodium and chlorine, most of these are present in a normal mixed ration or in green herbage plants, and it is not usually necessary to supply them separately. Salt licks or rock-salt lumps in the manger will supply the sodium and chlorine needed by the pony.

Vitamins are not really foods, but they are substances which the body requires if it is to function properly. They play different parts in digestion, growth, and development, and are very important in the young, rapidly growing animal. The principal vitamins and their chief functions are given in the table on the following page.

These three vitamins are each *fat soluble* and during times when an excess beyond immediate requirements is taken into the body, especially in spring and summer grazing, the excess is typically stored in the liver and in fat depôts, to be released later when necessary.

Name	Principal source	Chief functions
Vitamin A	Green plants, carrots, dried grass, lucerne or clover meals, fish-liver oils	To provide good growth in all body-tissue cells; to maintain normal strength in blood-vessel walls; to ensure good vision; to keep nerve cells healthy
Vitamin D	The sunlight; all sun-ripened foodstuffs; fish-liver oils	To stimulate and regulate all mineral absorption for bone and cartilage formation during growth, healing of fractures and repair of wounds
Vitamin E	The oil in the germ or embryos of most seeds, such as wheat, oats, barley, peas and beans. Also in small amounts in greenstuffs. Cold expressed wheat-germ oil	Maintains good muscle-cell function in the heart and skeletal muscles; is used by the reproductive organs during breeding and to build up muscle in the growing foal

The other vitamins, known as the *water-soluble* vitamins, are not able to be stored in the body and, though required in relatively smaller amounts, are quite important. The chief of them are as follows, though there are others of a very complex nature.

Name	Principal source	Chief functions
The B Vitamins	In most seeds, succulents and fruits	Used in digestion, nerve action, growth and to maintain normal growth of skin tissues and good supplies of blood cells
Vitamin C	Seeds, fruits and many fruit juices	To maintain general health, ward off disease, and repair damaged or wounded tissues

Name	Principal source	Chief functions
Vitamin K	Small amounts in many green and other foods	To maintain the integrity of the blood and ensure proper coagulation of blood after accident or disease

Each of these water-soluble vitamins, except C, has several members. Thus there are vitamins B_1, B_2, B_{12}, K, and K_1, which are fairly well known, and others whose nature and functions are highly complicated. Some of them are still undergoing investigation.

Chapter 3

FEEDING OF PONIES

The great majority of ponies are fed on naturally grown grass, hay and some amount of manger foods which include compounded cubes, oats, bran and chaff. Less commonly, various other foods, such as flaked maize, flaked wheat, barley either crushed or ground into a coarse meal, dried grass or dried lucerne, dried sugar beet pulp and so on, are used.

The commonest faults in pony feeding are that too much food is given and the pony becomes too fat, or that the feeding is erratic. Sometimes, e.g. during school term, the pony gets too little food and often too little exercise, while during holidays it gets too much, including numerous extras, tit-bits, cake, bread, sugar, sweets and so on. To some extent there is some common sense in this, because when the pony is not regularly ridden or worked it needs less than when in full work. However, on general sound principles there should not be either a feast or a famine succeeding each other.

Systems vary enormously and ponies possess great powers of adaptation. They can get used to almost any system provided no sudden changes are made. It is important to decide upon a system for both indoor and outdoor feeding and then to adhere to it as rigidly as circumstances will allow. Even when drastic changes are essential, these must be made gradually. This is discussed further later.

It is not uncommon to hear complaints that a newly

purchased pony does not settle down to feed regularly. On some days it feeds well; on others it leaves its trough feed and only picks at its hay. It is always a good plan to ask the seller or previous owner what system of feeding and management the pony had been given previously. When was the first feed given? Was water given before food? What amounts of corn and hay were being fed? Was the pony regularly worked or exercised each day, and for how long? When was the bulk of the long hay fed? When was the pony groomed? Was grazing allowed during the day and for how long? And so on.

The previous system may not be convenient for the new owner, but no harm will result if any necessary changes are made gradually.

It will be useful to discuss the foodstuffs separately before considering rations and feeding.

GRASS AND GRAZING

Grass varies enormously, from very poor to very good. Neither of these is good for the pony. Poor grass has a low nutritive value and is often mixed with weeds, some of which are harmful and some of which, while practically worthless in feeding, yet do no real harm if they are eaten. Top-quality grass, such as is grown and managed for feeding to dairy cows or to fattening bullocks, is too rich for normal ponies and, in addition to making them too fat, is very liable to cause laminitis ('founder', inflammation in the feet), to produce diarrhoea, gas fermentation in the bowels, or colic.

Ponies always do best on grass of average or medium quality, and this should always be chosen if at all possible. A reasonable amount of clover (wild white clover is best) among the grass plants is useful, but too much clover is just as bad as a rich 'cow' pasture.

One of the important functions of clover plants in a pasture is to fix atmospheric nitrogen, convert it into protein, and make it available for its own growth and also for the growth of the grasses situated near by. Indeed, this is the chief reason for including a small amount of clover when seeding down a new pasture to be used for grazing by horses.

Variations in quality

All pastures, the very good and the very poor, show marked variations in nutritive quality at different times of the year. The graphs herewith show in simplified manner the important variations which are typical through the various months of the year. It will be noted that in the months of May and June the protein and carbohydrate contents reach very high levels, and that in autumn the fibre contents are rising, in contrast to proteins, which reach their lowest levels in winter. This means that any average pasture has grass which changes upwards and downwards in nutritive value almost month by month. To some extent the natural appetite of a pony compensates for this variation; it eats less bulk in May and June per day, more in autumn, and more still in a winter day's grazing. However, it is a fact that practically all normal horses improve markedly in general condition when out at grass during May and June, and usually maintain this good condition during July and most of August, even later than this in some years.

Surplus growth of grass

In a pasture which is capable of providing for most of the needs of one pony during the winter months, there is always a surplus during spring and early summer, and to manage a paddock really properly necessitates some method of using up some of this surplus grass. The easiest plan is to arrange for perhaps two or three other ponies or two bullocks to be grazed on the paddock in addition for about 6 to 8 weeks of the spring 'flush' period. They should then be removed and the pony left by itself. Alternative methods consist of running a mowing machine over the paddock when the grass reaches about 6 or 8 inches in length so as to reduce it to about 2 inches long, which is probably the ideal length for spring and summer grazing by horses. Other methods are the use of a rotary mower, Hayter cutter, or gang-mower. A local farmer may be able to arrange to do this or have it done for small grazing paddocks used for ponies.

It may be necessary to repeat the cutting once or twice in an average year and even three times when the weather is especially warm and moist in a 'good growing year'. The cut stuff should be left lying on the pasture to dry and wilt, when much of it will be eaten later.

This may seem wasteful and unnecessary, but in fact keeping the grass short results in a gradual improvement in the total yield of grass during the season, and it is well worth carrying out if at all possible.

While long cut grass left lying on the pasture to dry hardly ever does any harm, a word of warning must be given against putting the fine cuttings from a lawn mower out onto a grazing pasture. Every year some ponies greedily eating lawn mowings become choked. They may get a severe colic and diarrhoea, and if not relieved by the veterinary surgeon as rapidly as possible, they may die. Lawn mowings are best made into a heap or put on a compost heap, to be dug in when they have become well rotted down.

c

Acreages per pony

The question is often asked: 'What size of paddock will be enough for one pony?' This is very hard to answer without knowing details. However, as a general guide where the paddock is to provide most of the food for 12 months, about $1\frac{1}{2}$ acres per pony is usually about correct for a pony up to about 14 hands, and $1\frac{3}{4}$ acres for a bigger pony of 15 hands. A Shetland or small crossbred of similar type will usually be kept fairly well on 1 acre. In each case the pasture should be of average grazing quality. As indicated above, these acreages will normally produce too much grass in the spring.

'Hay-on-the-stalk'

This phrase, used mostly in parts of the U.S.A., means that a pasture has been much undergrazed or not grazed at all during summer, the grass plants have put up flowering stalks, the seed has been shed, and what looks like stems of hay remain standing in the sward. The method is sometimes deliberately used to increase the grass plants from the ripe seed which falls and germinates. However, this needs careful management since the less useful or worthless grasses may be increased as well as the useful ones, and to be successful the method needs a good deal of knowledge of grass varieties and experience in grassland management. If it is to be undertaken, help and advice from a knowledgeable person should be sought.

Ponies often thrive well on an average pasture which has been allowed to develop 'hay-on-the-stalk'.

Varieties of grasses on grazing meadows

For those interested, it may be useful to include a brief classification of the commoner grasses of meadowlands. They are very difficult to identify except during their flowering periods. A botanical key will be useful.

Good grazing grasses

Perennial rye grasses—both early and late varieties (excellent)
Timothy grasses (excellent, but easily smothered by more vigorous types)
Smooth-stalked meadow grasses (good)
Annual meadow grass (good, but is annual only)
Most of the meadow fescues (useful)
Cocksfoot (the improved leafy strains)
Foxtails (useful as early bites in April and May)

Grasses of only medium grazing value

Crested dogstail (very palatable, poor yield of growth)
Sweet vernel (characteristic pleasant odour)
Brown wood grass (only eaten occasionally and when young)
Cocksfoots (the coarse unimproved tussocky strains)
Rough-stalked meadow grasses (not very palatable)
Bent grasses (only suitable on poorer land)

Poor or useless grasses

Yorkshire fog
Wall barley grass (also incorrectly called 'wild barley')
Sterile brome grass, and most other hard brome grasses
Couch grass
Wild oat grass
Sedges and cotton grasses (on hilly or moorland pastures, may be occasionally grazed when better types are absent)
Practically all the rushes (on waterlogged or swampy ground)

Strains

All over the world in the more advanced countries great improvements have been made in developing 'improved strains' of most of the grazing grasses during the last 30 years or so. Much of the early work was done by the late Sir George Stapledon and his colleagues at Aberystwyth. These improved strains are far superior in nutritive value and are generally known as 'pedigree strains'. They are identified by the letter 'S' and a number. For example, the pedigree perennial ryegrasses are known as S.23 and S.24; and the timothys are S.48 and S.50.

A carefully selected pedigree strain of any variety is always superior to a common or commercial strain of the same variety, and pastures formed by sowing these good strains provide more grass of better quality than when common (and cheaper) grass seeds are used, always provided that the mixture is well balanced, that the soil is of reasonable fertility and that the pasture is properly managed.

Methods of grazing

When ponies are turned out to grass and are left out day and night, they settle down to a sort of routine pattern of behaviour. They commence grazing at or soon after dawn and continue for about 2 or 3 hours. If the grass is dry as in summer, they break off and visit the water trough and drink about 1 to $1\frac{1}{2}$ gallons. They may then either graze again, but in the middle of the day seek shade and stand under a tree resting, especially if the biting flies are active. Some may lie and rest, half asleep, for 20 minutes to half an hour or so, then rise and graze again. When the worst of the mid-day sun is over, they may wander about the field eating a little here and there, probably drinking again, and in the evening settle down to graze steadily again until dusk or darkness falls. Then they choose a place to lie and rest. Two ponies which are companions will lie near each other; a mare and her young foal will lie quite near each other and usually a little distance from any other horses. In windy or cold weather, the ponies will nearly always seek some shelter and lie in the lee of a fence, wood, buildings or shelter belt; otherwise they will usually tend to sleep on the higher parts of a hilly pasture rather than in damp low-lying places.

Where there are several ponies running all together it is seldom that they all lie at the same time. One or two (or more) will stand on the edge of the others, apparently drowsing on their feet for 1 or 2 hours, then they will lie down and another (or others) will rise to their feet, stretch themselves, and then wander a short distance away and remain standing. It is possible that this behaviour pattern is inherited from wild ancestors and that the standing ponies are sentinels ready to give the alarm if danger or other disturbance threatens.

There are, of course, many variations of this general behaviour at grass. It is, however, very abnormal for any one pony to stay in one place in a paddock for long periods (e.g. hours) at a time. As mentioned earlier, the members of the horse tribe are all roamers and wanderers, moving about all over the grazing area, and any pony that stays in one place has something wrong with it and should be inspected. It may be lame or sick.

Selective grazing

All horses, but ponies in particular, soon find areas on an enclosed paddock, irrespective of size, where they tend to crop the herbage very short indeed and may eat out the grass almost bare, while in other areas, perhaps near by and separated by a sharply cut line, the grass plants are not eaten. Here the grass and weeds, etc., composing the sward, grow long, coarse and tussocky, and the pasture looks 'motheaten' and untidy. Further, it is in these coarse, over-grown areas that the majority of the ponies (but not all) tend to pass their dung. This adds extra fertility to these ungrazed areas and the plants become even stronger and coarser and a darker shade of green in consequence.

Efforts have been made to explain why some areas are so much more attractive than others, without success. The plants are the same, the soil is similar, often identical, and the reason is probably due to differences in palatability, taste or smell. The sensitive taste and smell organs in the pony's tongue and nostrils recognise differences which have quite eluded the efforts of the chemist and the analyst.

Some improvement in persuading ponies to eat the coarse rank ungrazed areas (which may be quite large in some paddocks) follows cutting the long coarse grass in May or June, sowing handfuls of coarse agricultural (or kitchen) salt at the rate of about $\frac{1}{2}$ lb. per square yard, first removing the dung if any considerable amount of it is present. Following this treatment the ponies will usually tend to eat the new young grass while it is fresh and succulent, but there is a tendency for the same pattern of selective grazing to recur in another year and the treatment has to be repeated. Sometimes, for unknown reasons every treatment fails.

Alternation of paddocks

It is always a good plan to have two or more paddocks available for the ponies wherever this is possible. Paddocks which are too large can be split into two or more by a fence, e.g. a 4-acre paddock may be divided into three parts of about $1\frac{1}{4}$ to $1\frac{1}{2}$ acres each. Normally a paddock for one pony should not be less than about 1 to $1\frac{1}{2}$ acres in size if it is to be used throughout the year, but a great deal depends on the type and quality of the grass, the situation, and how much extra feeding can be given.

HAYS

After grazing, hay is the next most important food required by the pony. Hays available for purchase vary enormously in composition and nutritive quality. At the top level there is first-class *seeds hay*, clean and well harvested, grown on rich, fertile land, and usually composed of a good grass, such as Italian ryegrass mixed with red or white clover. Pure hays of clover (often called 'stuvver'), sainfoin or lucerne are grown, but they are normally too rich and 'heating' for ponies, though they are occasionally used for hard-working show ponies. They must be introduced with care and only used in sparing amounts.

Of the *seeds hays*, ordinary commercially grown kinds are safer and better for ponies, and many farmers are prepared to sell a few trusses of their own ryegrass and clover mixture for a reasonable price to a pony owner. It is best bought in trusses, which are generally of about the same weight (usually around 50 to 56 lb.), and by using trusses, string-tied rather than wire-tied if possible, a fairly good check can be kept on the amount consumed per week. If 8 lb. per day are fed, a truss should last a week. Costs vary greatly, but from about 7s. 6d. to about 10s. per truss should be a realistic amount to pay (1968) for a fair average sample.

Meadow hays are made from permanent meadows and are not the result of sowing seed for a hay crop as are seeds hays. They are composed of the blades and stems of whatever grasses and other plants grow on the meadow, which is shut up and cut for hay instead of being grazed. A good sample will always have more dried blades of the grasses and fewer stems and flowering heads. Most permanent pastures grown on reasonably good soil contain a proportion of wild white clovers, trefoils and sometimes other legumes. These when dried in the hay are palatable and add to the feeding value of the hay. A reasonable and average percentage of about 20 to 30 per cent is probably best.

These hays also vary much in composition and nutritive value, and good or average meadow hays are probably the best and safest types to choose for feeding a pony, and many mature ponies can keep quite well and healthy on grass and good average hay throughout the greater part of the year. Young growing ponies under 3 years old, mares with foal at foot and any pony being ridden daily or when being prepared for showing, jumping, etc., require more food nutriment than is available from grass and hay, if it is to be kept in hard, fit working condition.

Hay from rough-pasture, road verges, or waste land is sometimes sold to unsuspecting pony owners. An occasional sample may be fair, but by and large this type of hay is of poor or very poor value, often mixed with weeds, wild flowers, roadside rubbish, etc., and it is better avoided. This same remark applies even more to samples which are blackish, dusty, stale, badly spoilt by rain after cutting, mouldy, wet or mowburnt (dark chocolate brown from over-heating and partial charring in the stack). Feeding on such samples, if indeed the ponies will eat them at all, is risky because they easily cause indigestion, colic, diarrhoea sometimes and, especially when mouldy, a serious kidney disturbance (polyuria) with wasting of muscles and loss of condition subsequently.

Amounts to feed

Much will depend upon what other foods, grazing or concentrates, are being fed and whether the pony is in hard regular work (e.g. during school holidays) or resting. The following quantities are to be regarded as the amounts to feed when hay is a principal food, though not necessarily the only one.

Best-quality seeds hays

For a 300-lb. pony   4 to 6 lb. per day
For a 400-lb. pony   6 to 7 lb. per day
For a 600-lb. pony   8 to 9 lb. per day

Medium, soft average meadow hays

For a 300-lb. pony   5 to 6 or 7 lb. per day
For a 400-lb. pony   6 to 8 lb. per day
For a 600-lb. pony   9 to 10 lb. per day

Poor inferior-quality hay (but capable of providing some food)

For a 300-lb. pony   6 to 8 or 9 lb. per day
For a 400-lb. pony   9 to 10 or 11 lb. per day
For a 600-lb. pony   10 to 12 or 13 lb. per day

It will be noted that in terms of amounts per live weight of pony, the quantities vary from about $1\frac{1}{3}$ lb. for best hay to $2\frac{1}{2}$ or 3 lb. for poor hay for each 100 lb. the pony weighs.

As general guides, the following points are worth keeping in mind. If a pony finishes its hay and then begins to eat the straw of its bedding, it is getting less hay (roughage) than it requires. Conversely, if the hay is sound and the pony does not eat it readily and leaves some untouched, it is getting too much and the daily amount must be reduced. This is simple common sense, but then common sense is one of the most important assets to have or to cultivate by all who wish to keep animals of any sort.

OATS

Oats as used for feeding are the ripe seeds of the cereal plant *Avena sativa* which is extensively grown in temperate and

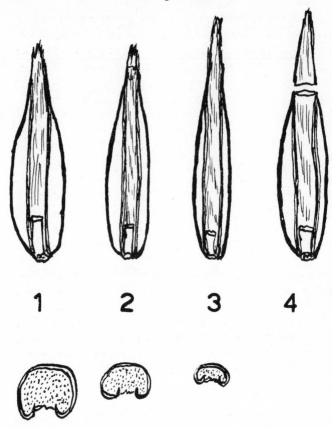

Fig. 5. Diagram to illustrate differences in types of oats. 1, a fat plump 'potato' oat; 2, an ordinary medium type of oat; 3, a long thin slender oat; 4, a clipped oat.

The cross-sections of each oat below show how much more of the endosperm, containing starches, proteins and fats (shown stippled), is contained within the fibrous husk. In 3, the proportion of husk to endosperm is far higher and therefore the nutritive value is lower per lb. weight when used for feeding.

cool countries. Oats are by tradition the most commonly used food as a concentrate for horses and ponies in Britain, and indeed in most temperate parts of the world. They are fed either whole, crushed or rolled, some people preferring one type and some another. So long as it is borne in mind that a 'bowlful' of crushed oats weighs materially less than a 'bowlful' of whole oats, and so long as the *weight* of the oats fed per day is the same, it does not really matter whether the oats are whole or crushed (see p. 39).

Oats are composed of an outer fibrous coat or husk that encloses the kernel, which consists essentially of the germ of the seed and the endosperm—a store of starch upon which the new young plant lives after germination has taken place.

Oats as a crop grow best on fertile soil in a climate where the conditions during the growing season are fundamentally cool and moist, with a period of dry weather after the crop has finished growing and is ripening, and during harvesting operations. The richer 'carse lands' of Scotland's valleys fulfil these conditions better than the traditionally heavy clay soils in much of England, where wheat and barley grow better. Much of Scotland's best oats go to the makers of porridge oats and oatmeals for human consumption; others are bought by the owners of racehorse studs and the big training stables at prices which are usually more than the pony owner can afford.

All this means that ponies do not usually get the best Scottish or 'potato' oats, but it is good advice to recommend that the oats bought for the pony should be the best that can be afforded. Less amounts will be needed per day; supplies will last longer, and the ultimate cost per year will not be so very different from feeding on cheaper, poor-quality oats. Further, the pony will do better, keep more healthy and be fitter for its work.

How to judge good oats (whole)

The oats should be taken up by the handful, spread out and looked at carefully. The general colours should be a dull pale golden colour (white oats), pale silver-grey (grey oats) or dark chocolate brownish black (black oats). There should be a good degree of uniformity in size and shape between individual grains; too many small grains means that the sample has not been properly screened to remove the small 'seconds' or 'thirds'. The presence of these by themselves is not so important (except that they lower the nutritive value of the sample), but imperfectly screened samples also contain weed seeds, sometimes dried mud or perhaps small stones or mouse dung in small blackish pellets. These are all very undesirable in a sample of oats to be used for pony feeding.

When buying oats purchasers should not be persuaded by dealers to accept parcels of oats which they cannot sell to owners of hunters or other horses, by saying: 'Oh well, these oats are good enough for ponies, which do not need good oats.'

When examined, each oat should be plump and short rather than thin and elongated. The point of the oat may have a short bristle, but long narrow points are always associated with a higher than normal fibre content. While fibre is essential for good digestion, it is better to use hay than the much more expensive oats as the source of it.

The oats should feel hard and dry, slipping over each other without any stickiness. There should be no sour, stale, sickly or unpleasant smell. The colour should be clean and uniform; there should be no dustiness, weather-staining, mouldiness or mustiness, and there should be no admixture with mud, small stones, weed seeds, or rat or mouse dung.

If a single representative oat grain is cut through with a knife, or is peeled free from its husk, the endosperm or starch stored in the kernel should be of a clean chalky-white appearance. If chewed, the taste should be first somewhat mealy or nutty and then quite appreciably sweet, and the sweeter the chewed kernel becomes, the better the sample is likely to be. Any bitterness, sourness or other unpleasant taste usually means that moulds have invaded the kernel, or that the oats were cut before they were properly ripe.

Considerable experience is needed to be able to judge a sample properly, and it is a good plan for young people to see as many different samples of oats as possible, and discuss them with friends and experts whenever possible.

From a practical point of view the only really useful quick test of the goodness or otherwise of a sample of oats is to determine the weight of a bushel measure.

Weight per bushel

A buyer can always ask for this weight and can check it himself if necessary. A good sample should weigh 42 lb. per bushel; 40 lb. is passable, even down to 38 lb. can be accepted. Weights of 36 lb. per bushel or less than this should not be bought for ponies; they are often of very poor value, poor in starch, containing far too much fibre, and often have quantities of rubbish in them. For the sake of contrast, the best potato oats may weigh 46, 48, and prize samples as much as 50 lb. per bushel.

Whole versus crushed oats

There is some advantage in feeding oats which have been crushed, rolled or bruised to horses, in particular to young growing animals or the very old, but there are certain conditions. The oats should be freshly crushed. After about 7

SAMPLES OF OATS FOR COMPARISON

All have been photographed to the same scale; lighting and exposures were constant.

Fig. 6. A good sound healthy sample of oats. Grains are all full and plump; colour is bright and uniform; there are no damaged, weathered

Fig. 7. Sample of well-grown but badly harvested oats. The grains of good and fairly uniform size are nearly all tinged with greyish or darkish stain, discoloration from wet weather at harvest time.

Samples like this, provided they show no mould growth, are satisfactory for feeding, but are usually a little less palatable than a good sample, as in Fig. 6. They sometimes taste slightly bitter if chewed for a minute or two.

Fig. 8. Two samples of small oats, probably first screenings from oats for porridge making. The *left* one shows small but sound grains which are satisfactory but of rather lower feeding value. Weight per bushel, 40 lb. The *right* is a similar sample, but has been somewhat 'weathered'. Dark staining shows on some of the grains. Also of lowered feeding value.

Fig. 9. This is also a fairly good sample, but some grains are slightly stained and weathered. This happens when rain at harvest soaks the outside of the sheaves, but the centres remain dry and unaffected. The scale is in millimetres and gives a measure of sizes. Weight per bushel: 41 lb.

D

Fig. 10. Sample of rolled oats. The smaller grains escape being broken by the heavy rollers, but the larger, plumper grains are rolled and broken to expose the kernels (endosperm). Some have lost their husks.

Oats which have been rolled or crushed begin to deteriorate in feeding value and should be used within a week of crushing or rolling. Otherwise they begin to grow sour and stale, and their nutritive value is depressed.

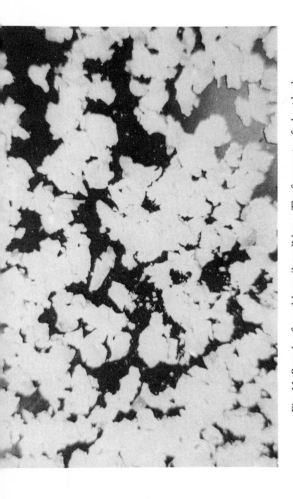

Fig. 11. Sample of good large 'broad' bran. The fragments of wheat husk are large, clean and tasty to the pony. There is a minimum of small broken pieces, meal or dust. This is the best type of bran for feeding or from which to make bran mashes, but it is often difficult to obtain on the market.

Ordinary bran has much smaller fragments, more meal and looks more 'dusty'. It is, however, perfectly satisfactory if good 'broad' bran is not available.

days, the nutritive value of the crushed oats begins to deteriorate, at first only slowly, but more rapidly after a period of about 15 to 18 days onwards. Once the oat has been crushed it is no longer a living individual; the crushing kills it and everything living which is deprived of life begins to decompose and to go rotten.

An excellent rule is to have the oats crushed once weekly and to use up each week's supply before any more is crushed.

Adult horses of all kinds which have normal mature teeth are perfectly able to chew whole oats, and will do well on them. On the other hand, crushed oats are a little more easily chewed and swallowed and mix with the saliva and other digestive juices more quickly. Tests have shown that crushed oats have about 5 per cent advantage over whole oats on a pound to pound basis. The importance of feeding *by weight* instead of by 'bowlful', which is a very variable quantity, must be stressed.

BRAN

Bran is the husk of the wheat grain, which is separated during milling for wheat flour. The grain is ground between powerful rollers, and the result is sieved through successively small sieves. The coarsest sieve removes the larger husk flakes, which constitute broad bran. Smaller sieves remove the finer particles which are sold under a variety of names, viz. middlings, sharpes, wheatings or weetings.

These are mainly used for pig, poultry or calf feeding. The finest particles, which pass through the smallest sieve (often made of silk or nylon net), are the flour grains which are, of course, used for bread-making, cakes, pastry, biscuits and so on, for human feeding.

Bran is a useful food for horses and ponies, but its uses are often misunderstood. Bran possesses a good deal of fibre, but it is softer and more digestible than the husk of the oat. It contains an inner layer of cells which contain the vitamins present in the wheat grain, known as the *aleurone layer*, and it is rich in phosphorus. Bran suits the horses' intestinal system very well, and the value of a bran mash once a week or so is well known (see p. 48). Dry bran often tends to be used in too big a proportion along with crushed oats; as a general rule bran should be used in the proportions of one part to four of the crushed oats. It is a mistake to feed too much bran for a long period of time, because it is poor in calcium and magnesium and far too rich in phosphorus, and leads to a mineral imbalance. This is of most importance in foals and young growing ponies. The unbalanced minerals result in poor bone growth and development.

In the correct proportions with other foods and hay, bran is a valuable and important foodstuff in spite of what is said above.

Bran mashes have the advantage that they are very palatable, well tolerated by the intestines, and if made properly have undergone softening and some degree of pre-digestion. They are very important for sick or convalescent ponies of any age as a form of 'sick-feeding'. They have a gentle laxative action preventing constipation and have a soothing action on inflamed or irritated mucous membranes. Ponies in full work on a heavy ration benefit greatly by having a bran mash at week-ends. On Saturday mornings feed only half the normal concentrate ration, give hay only at midday, and in the evening give the bran mash instead of the concentrates (oats, etc.). Feed hay afterwards to be eaten overnight.

Bran mashes should be properly made and it takes about

1 hour or sometimes a little longer before they are ready to be fed.

To make a bran mash

Obtain a galvanised bucket of about 2 gallons capacity, a gallon of *boiling* water preferably in a large kettle, about 2 oz. of coarse common kitchen salt, a stick to stir, a large stout sack and a supply of bran.

Put about a feeding bowlful and a half (1 to $1\frac{1}{2}$ lb.) of bran into the bucket, and the 2 oz. of common salt. Add 1 gallon of really boiling, scalding hot water and stir well. Cover the bucket up with the sack (a thick corn sack is best) and allow to stand for about 40 minutes or until it has cooled down so that it is only comfortably hot to the hand. Test the heat after a thorough stir so that the hottest parts in the centre are well mixed and distributed. Then tip into the manger and let the pony eat it. For a sick pony, add a handful or two of crushed oats and a teacupful of treacle or treacle water (1 to 4 of water). These will often encourage a pony whose appetite is a little tricky to eat the mash with more eagerness.

There are two general precautions. Be sure the mash is thoroughly stirred and is left long enough to soak properly and that it is not too hot when fed. Afterwards be sure that the manger is washed and cleaned. Any mash not eaten and left in the manger becomes sour and rancid in about 6 hours and taints the manger so that the pony may only pick or refuse its food next day.

To make a linseed mash

A double-walled sauce-pan or stew-pan, the inner container holding a gallon or more, is most convenient, but not essential. If a single-walled pot is used, more stirring is needed to avoid burning. Take about $\frac{3}{4}$ gallon of clean water, mix about $\frac{1}{4}$ lb. of clean washed whole linseeds, bring to the boil and boil vigorously for 10 to 15 minutes by the clock, stirring thoroughly. This is necessary to destroy the enzyme present in raw linseed, which would otherwise generate prussic acid by acting on the glucosides. Then reduce the heat and simmer gently for 5 to 6 hours, stirring occasionally. Allow to cool. Feed along with the whole of the fluids ('the linseed tea'), which are nutritionally very valuable. Add a little extra water if necessary to maintain volume.

Never mix boiled and unboiled linseed mash or other linseed products together. Cold linseed mash is unpalatable and goes stale and sour in about 5 hours. Clean out the manger and discard any mash not eaten after this time.

Other mashes

Sometimes instead of bran only, a mixture of about equal parts of crushed oats and bran is useful. This is rather more nourishing. Bran 1 part, crushed barley 1 part and crushed oats 1 part makes another useful mash which may be fed twice or even three times weekly to a pony which has lost much condition from illness. A very palatable mash can also be made of equal parts of flaked maize, crushed oats and bran, or a handful or two of flaked maize may be added after scalding and just before feeding. Porridge made from Quaker oats as for human use can be stirred into a bran mash. About $1\frac{1}{2}$ to 2 pints of porridge is about the correct amount. This is useful for a pony which has, or has had, diarrhoea.

Other useful mashes can be made by mixing a small linseed mash made separately, into a bran mash just before feeding, and various succulents, *well cut up or sliced* to avoid risk of choking, such as apples, carrots, parsnips, swedes, mangels, etc., can be added to the bran mash and well stirred through it. **Never add raw linseeds to a bran mash or to any mash containing any linseed product.**

For special purposes your veterinary surgeon may advise certain other kinds of mashes, some containing drugs or medicine. He will give directions for making them. Either Glauber's or Epsom salts in amounts of 3 to 4 oz. to each mash are useful where a sick pony has become very constipated, dry and hard in its faeces. This is liable to occur when a pony is receiving too much dry hay and because of illness is not able to be given enough exercise.

Caution: Always remember three things regarding mashes:

(1) They must be thoroughly scalded and left covered for at least 30 to 40 minutes.
(2) They must not be too hot when given to the pony.
(3) Any residue of mash remaining in the manger 4 to 6 hours later must be removed before it becomes fermented, stale or sour, and taints the manger or future food placed in it.

Chapter 4

DIFFERENCES IN CANADA AND THE U.S.A.

While the *principles* of feeding described apply with slight modifications to ponies kept in all countries with a temperate climate, there are some local differences which may be mentioned and which may be found useful.

In Canada and some parts of the U.S.A. the long period of winter makes it difficult to ensure enough exercise and to avoid over-feeding. The ponies are usually kept in horse barns and should be given the biggest boxes that are available. They will then get more room to walk about and will take some exercise automatically. Two ponies which are used to each other can be put in one large box. At least once a day it is a good plan to exercise them by walking them or riding them up and down the long central passage-way which in most barns runs the whole length of the building. Whenever the weather allows they should be got out into the open air even though the ground is still covered with some inches of snow.

It is perhaps even more important than in warmer parts to ensure that minerals and vitamins are included in proper amounts in the winter rations. Many good pelleted foods, cubes and similar compounds sold locally contain adequate amounts of these substances.

ALFALFA HAYS

In many parts of both North and South America, alfalfa (lucerne) is grown extensively and is used either as dry

51

roughage or is incorporated into cubes and pellets for horse feeding. Dried alfalfa meal made from green cut alfalfa is used in these compound mixtures. It is richer in vitamin A and in calcium, pound for pound, than is alfalfa hay.

When alfalfa hay is fed as a roughage instead of a cereal hay, some care is needed. It is richer in protein than most timothy, Bermuda grass, prairie grass, brome or other similar hays, and therefore less is needed per day. When alfalfa hay has been cut late after flowering (to get a heavier cut per acre), it tends to become very much more coarse and fuller of hard woody stems. Many of the richer green leaves are shattered off by handling, and very coarse alfalfa hay may give rise to indigestion and impaction of the double colon if it is eaten in too large amounts. Ponies usually eat it readily enough, but being hard and woody it is not chewed properly. An oldish pony with worn teeth is likely to suffer more than a younger one. Alfalfa hay should be introduced into the pony's rations only in small amounts for the first week or ten days, until it gets used to it.

For an idle pony only about $\frac{3}{4}$ to 1 lb. of alfalfa hay per 100 lb. live weight per day is needed, even when little or no other food is fed. If it is very dusty when handled, sprinkling with clean water or with treacle (molasses) water immediately before feeding will make it a little more palatable.

CONCENTRATES

Cubes and pelleted foods are much used across the Atlantic, possibly more than in anywhere else in the world. Most of them are good, and there is no doubt that they have come to stay (see also page 54). The actual ingredients vary considerably. In addition to oats, barley and wheat brans, most cubes contain different maize products; some have proportions of soya-bean meal (very useful for the in-foal or nursing mare and the young growing foal), sorghums (millets or milo), various mineral and vitamin additives, and as mentioned very many contain dried green alfalfa or clover meals. Treacle or molasses is used to bind the dry ingredients in most cubes and pellets, and these, being sweet, contribute to increased palatability. A few cubes contain ginger or other spices and are reputed to act as mild tonics for a pony with a jaded appetite. On the whole they are probably not necessary.

PASTURES

As in most countries, grazing pastures form the biggest source of food supply for ponies in all areas where it is possible to establish good species of grasses. The actual varieties of grasses however are often different. Some which are used locally are not available elsewhere. Kentucky blue grass and wild white clovers is a well-known mixture for horse paddocks in the U.S.A., especially for Thoroughbreds. Other grazing pastures contain pure stands of Kentucky blue grass, various fescues, prairie grasses and even alfalfa, or mixtures of these. An effort is always made to construct a mixture of grasses and herbs which will give as long a period of grazing as possible, from the 'early bite' in spring to the late autumn flush in the 'back end' of the year.

Chapter 5

CUBES AND CUBE-FEEDING

Cakes and cubes have been used for feeding to cattle, sheep and even pigs and poultry for many years past, but it is only during the last 12 or 14 years that they have been specially compounded for feeding to horses and ponies.

Cubes are a convenient way of ensuring a more regular composition in the horse's food, not subject to variations due to bad weather, poor harvests, wide differences in prices from year to year and often difficulty in obtaining regular supplies.

Much thought and work have gone into the manufacture of the better types of pony cubes, and it can be confidently stated that when these are made by a reliable firm which has a good reputation to maintain, they can be fully recommended for feeding to riding ponies, provided they are sensibly used.

Pellets and cubes as a complete food for ponies

Much attention has been paid to the possibility of compounding a type of cube which could be used as the sole food on which to feed a horse or pony. If this could be done it might dispense with the need to feed hay, oats, bran or anything else, and there are some lazy owners who would like to be able to feed cubes and nothing else. It is the author's opinion, in the light of our present knowledge of the peculiar structure and functions of the horse's digestive system, that it would be fundamentally wrong to feed ponies on nothing but cubes, no matter how these were constructed and compounded. The pony obtains a long period of mental and physical relaxation contentedly eating and chewing long hay, a free flow of saliva occurs during chewing which plays an important part in digestion, while the importance of a sufficiency of fibrous roughage in intestinal digestion has already been discussed (see p. 19). Where so-called 'complete ration' cubes have been fed experimentally, apart from the actual composition difficulties, the cubes are nearly always eaten far too quickly, and the pony's appetite is not properly satisfied. Cubes are tasty, easily broken up into fragments which can be readily swallowed without prolonged chewing, and are nearly always eaten quickly. A pony which gobbles up its cube ration in about 20 to 30 minutes has nothing to do during the long hours when it would otherwise be slowly and regularly munching its hay. To satisfy its need for bulky roughage and to give itself something to do, a pony on 'all cube' feeding starts to eat its bedding, chews the woodwork of door or manger, some have developed the vices of 'crib-biting' or 'wind-sucking', while a few have learnt to chew their own tails in an effort to find the roughage they require. These vices, if they are allowed to become established, are very hard to overcome, and may lead to loss of condition, inability to stand up to reasonable work, and may encourage the development of lung trouble.

When, however, good-quality reliable cubes are fed as part of the rations, none of these disadvantages follow.

Different ways of feeding cubes

There is some difference of opinion as to whether a pony should get cubes and hay (or grazing) and no crushed oats and bran, or whether the ration should contain at least some crushed oats and bran. Much depends upon the management

of the pony and how it is exercised and for what purpose
the pony is kept.

To illustrate the *worst way* to feed cubes, a short descrip-
tion of how deaths may arise from wrong cube feeding may
be mentioned. Three young horses being prepared for showing later in the year were being grazed on good grass daily
in late May. They were turned out about 8 a.m. and brought
in after mid-day. They were getting 2 lb. of cubes on coming
in, along with long hay. Then the system was unfortunately
suddenly changed. The horses each got their cubes *before*
going out to grass and ate them greedily. For 3 or 4 days
no harm resulted, probably because the weather was dry.
Then there was rain overnight, and the next day two horses
were seen to be dull and off food at mid-day and one died
that same evening with severe colic. The second gradually
recovered, and the third was only slightly affected. Post-
mortem examination of the dead animal showed a burst
stomach, and death occurred from peritonitis and shock.
The stomach was packed with a thick doughy mass of
crushed-up cubes and a little wet grass which together had
rapidly fermented, giving off much gas.

Clearly what had happened was that the horses had eaten
their cubes on an empty stomach and then, when turned out,
settled down to eat the sweet and luscious wet grass. The
moisture and warmth had resulted in rapid fermentation, and
the controlling digestive juices (which normally should have
arrested this fermentation) were unable to penetrate the
pasty doughy mass of ground-down cubes.

A very important lesson should be learnt from this un-
fortunate episode, which is the reason for recounting it. If
these young animals had been given a small feed of long hay,
chaff, oats or other dry fibrous material *before* eating the
cubes, or along with them, there is little or no chance that

they would have suffered from grazing the wet grass, even though they had eaten it greedily. Their stomachs would have contained enough fibre to break up the chewed cubes and to mix with the mass, preventing it from setting into a pasty tenacious mass, and rapid fermentation would not have occurred.

With the pony cubes available at present on the market, there is more fibre than in the richer 'stud cubes', but the dangers of an 'all-cube' mass in the stomach are still there. The recommendation is made that even when only 2 or 3 lb. of cubes are being fed to a pony daily, they should never be given alone on an empty stomach, and water to drink should always be given before feeding.

Chapter 6

AMOUNTS TO FEED

General considerations

This is perhaps the most difficult matter upon which to write. Let it be said at the outset that one cannot feed ponies successfully by working out rigid arithmetic rations, and then feeding hard-and-fast amounts per day. Every pony must be studied as an individual and fed accordingly. Some will become too fat on a given ration, while others may lose flesh on the same ration. The age of the pony, the kind and amount of work or exercise it performs, the character and efficiency of the teeth and of the digestive system, freedom from disease or worm parasites, and other factors, each has an influence upon whether a pony does well, thrives and grows upon a given feeding system or whether it does not.

Before giving details, it is strongly recommended that each pony's likes or dislikes, its methods of feeding—greedy, lazy, or otherwise—should be studied in as much detail as possible. With a newly purchased pony, always ask what its feeding has been and whether it has any peculiarities in feeding. If a pony is slow in eating, it may have an abnormality in its mouth or throat; if it puts some of its food out of its mouth into the manger, it may have some trouble in its teeth; if it eats a little food greedily and then stops for a minute or two, it may have difficulty in swallowing. In these cases, a veterinary surgeon should be consulted and an examination of mouth, teeth, throat, etc., may disclose the reason.

Additionally, when drinking water, small amounts are sometimes discharged through the nostrils, which usually indicates muscular abnormality in the muscles of the throat. An occasional pony cannot (or does not) drink with its lips and mouth, but plunges its muzzle into the water so that the nostrils are below the surface. This does not seem to matter, but the pony lifts its head from the bucket or water trough at frequent intervals to take a few breaths of air, and takes much longer to satisfy its thirst. It needs plenty of time. Very rarely a pony will lap like a dog or cat, but manages quite satisfactorily.

Some ponies, when fed on a mixture of oats or cubes and chaffed hay, learn to root the lighter chaff out of the manger onto the floor, and then eat the tastier crushed oats or cubes greedily, perhaps without proper chewing. This may lead to indigestion or even colic immediately after a feed.

Daily amounts

1. *For working conditions*

		Concentrates* (lb.)	Hay (lb.)	Grazing hours† daily
(a)	Shetlands	1½–2	4–5	3–4
(b)	Welsh Mountain	2–3	5–7	4
(c)	Exmoor, Dartmoor, Fells and Dales	Up to 4	7–8	4
(d)	Arab × Pony crosses	5–6	10–11	4
(e)	Connemara and other large types	6 or more	12–14	4

2. *When not working, but indoors at night-time, out during the day*

(a)	Shetlands	—	5 (evening)	8
(b)	Welsh Mountain	—	6	8
(c)	Exmoors, etc.	—	8	8
(d)	Arab crosses	1–2	10	8
(e)	Connemara, etc.	2	12	8

3. *After being turned out then being got up for about 2–3 weeks before work commences*

(a) Shetlands	1	4	3–4
(b) Welsh Mountain	2	5	3–4
(c) Exmoors, etc.	2–3	6–7	3–4
(d) Arab crosses	4	8–10	3–4
(e) Connemara	5	10–12	3–4

* These may be either crushed oats and bran mixture of about 4 to 1, pony cubes of good quality or mixtures of these.

† Under most practical conditions, this usually means a forenoon or an afternoon out to grass, the pony being exercised, worked or attending rallies, shows, etc., for the other part of the day.

These amounts are obviously approximate and are to be regarded as starting points which may be gradually increased or reduced as circumstances require. Good-quality foods are assumed. Where poor-quality oats and hay are fed or inferior grazing only is available, the amounts may have to be increased by about 10 to 15 per cent per day.

It cannot be too strongly emphasised that the above tables are to be regarded as guides only. Some ponies are much more efficient converters of food than others and are easily able to keep themselves in good condition on less food than others. These ponies of any breed or type need less than the amounts indicated above.

Finally, a plea must be made for the exercise of constant observation and supervision of all details of each pony's feeding and drinking habits, likes and dislikes, and other idiosyncrasies. Learn all you can about your pony and be prepared to make allowances when these are required.

Where necessary further advice in specific cases should be obtained from your veterinary surgeon or from someone who is fully experienced. Never hesitate to ask for advice; most people who are competent to do so will be found very willing to advise and help.